# AN Egyptian TOMB

Meredith Hooper

FIREFLY BOOKS

# A FIREFLY BOOK

Published by Firefly Books Ltd. 2008

First printing

**Publisher Cataloging-in-Publication Data (U.S.)**

Hooper, Meredith.
    An Egyptian tomb : the tomb of Nebamun / Meredith Hooper.
[32] p. : col. ill., col. photos. ;   cm.
Includes index.
Summary: Explores the mysteries of the tomb of the ancient Egyptian Nebamun through the recently conserved paintings of his tomb-chapel.
ISBN-13: 978-1-55407-374-0
ISBN-10: 1-55407-374-X
1. Tombs — Egypt —Thebes (Extinct city) — Juvenile literature.  2. Egypt —History — To 332 B.C. — Juvenile literature.  3. Nebamun — Juvenile literature. I. Title.
932 dc22   DT62.T6.H667  2008

**Library and Archives Canada Cataloguing in Publication**

Hooper, Meredith
    An Egyptian tomb : the tomb of Nebamun / Meredith Hooper.
Includes index.
ISBN-13: 978-1-55407-374-0
ISBN-10: 1-55407-374-X
    1. Nebamun—Tomb—Juvenile literature.  2. Tombs—Egypt—Juvenile literature.  I. Title.
DT62.T6H66 2008        j932'.01      C2007-905696-2

Published in the United States by
Firefly Books (U.S.) Inc.
P.O. Box 1338, Ellicott Station
Buffalo, New York 14205

Published in Canada by
Firefly Books Ltd.
66 Leek Crescent
Richmond Hill, Ontario L4B 1H1

Designed and typeset by Price Watkins

Printed in China

# To my daughter Rachel

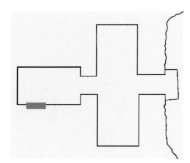

**Author's acknowledgements**

The author wishes to acknowledge the invaluable assistance of Dr Richard Parkinson of the Department of Ancient Egypt and Sudan, British Museum, in the research and the writing of this book.

Dr Parkinson's book, *The Painted Tomb-Chapel of Nebamun: Masterpieces of Ancient Egyptian Art*, British Museum Press, 2008, is recommended to adult readers wishing to find out more about the Nebamun paintings.

**Illustration acknowledgements**

Photographs of the Nebamun paintings were taken by Kevin Lovelock of the British Museum Photography and Imaging Department, © The Trustees of the British Museum.
Photographs of other British Museum objects were taken by the British Museum Photography and Imaging Department,  © The Trustees of the British Museum.
Illustrations on pages 6–7 and 8 by Chris Molan.
Illustration on pages 10–11 by Dr Richard Parkinson.
Photograph on pages 12–13 by Dr José Galán, "Projecto Djehuty", Spanish-Egyptian Mission at Dra Abu el-Naga.
Photographs on pages 14–15 by Dr Lise Manniche.
Reconstruction drawings on pages 18-19, 20, 21, 22–23, 24– 25, and 26 –27 by Claire Thorne and Richard Parkinson.

**The paintings**

The paintings you see in this book are now in the British Museum. Everything in the Museum has a special number that allows people to find it. The numbers of the paintings are:
EA 37979 Nebamun sitting on a chair
EA 37977 Hunting in the marshes
EA 37983 Garden pond
EA 37980 Servants carrying hares
EA 37985 Table piled with food offerings
EA 37984, 37981 and 37986 Party scenes
EA 37978 Geese
EA 37976 Cattle
EA 37982 Chariots and horses
The painting on page 1 is a detail of Nebamun's wife (see page 17 for the whole picture).

This is a plan of Nebamun's tomb. You can find this plan next to some of the paintings in this book. A blue line shows which wall of the tomb the painting was once on. Visitors to the tomb would have seen the painting of servants carrying hares in the inner room.

# Contents

# Who was Nebamun?

Nebamun was an official in the Temple of Amun in the city of Thebes, beside the river Nile. He lived nearly 3,500 years ago in ancient Egypt.

The people who knew how to read and write in Egypt were called scribes. There were few of them – most people could not read or write.

Nebamun was a scribe. He kept a record of the grain grown on the Temple's farms. Grain was like money. Nebamun paid people for their work in grain.

Nebamun wanted a beautiful tomb where his body would be kept safely after he died. Nebamun wasn't very important. He wasn't very rich. But he knew the right people.

**Nebamun sits on a chair with a panther-skin spread over the seat.**

Hacking a room out of solid rock is very expensive. Getting the best artists to paint pictures on the walls costs a lot.

Nebamun paid for two rooms wide enough to stretch out his arms without touching the walls, and high enough not to bump his head on the ceiling. The artists covered the walls with paintings of Nebamun being busy, and happy. They painted his family and friends, and some of the people who worked for him.

**This is Nebamun's wife, Hatshepsut.**

**This is his daughter.**

**And here is Nebamun's cat.**

The Egyptians wrote in picture-signs called hieroglyphs. Most hieroglyphs stood for sounds but some stood for a word.

**This reads 'Nebamun'.**

**This reads 'Hatshepsut'.**

5

Workmen dug into the hillside to make Nebamun's tomb. They cut away the rock to hollow out two rooms and a passage, using hammers of stone and chisels of bronze.

Plasterers chopped up straw from the fields and mixed it through coarse brown mud scooped from the river Nile. They pushed the mixture of straw and mud on to the rough walls with their fingers in a thick squishy smelly layer. When the brown mud was dry and hard they smoothed a thin layer of white plaster over the top, like icing on a ginger cake.

As soon as the plaster was dry the artists began to paint.

They used brushes, as well as rushes, chewing the ends to make them soft.

First the artists drew the outlines of each picture. For some scenes they marked squares on the walls, using the squares to get everything in the right place. Next, they filled in the colours – blue for water, red for men's skin, black for hair and eyes, white for clothes, green for plants. The coloured paint went straight on to the plaster. Last of all, everything was given another outline.

It was quite dark inside the tomb. The artists painted by lamplight. Probably five or six artists worked together, but we do not know their names.

The artists used red, yellow, green, blue, black and white paints. Each colour was kept in a pot or a shell.

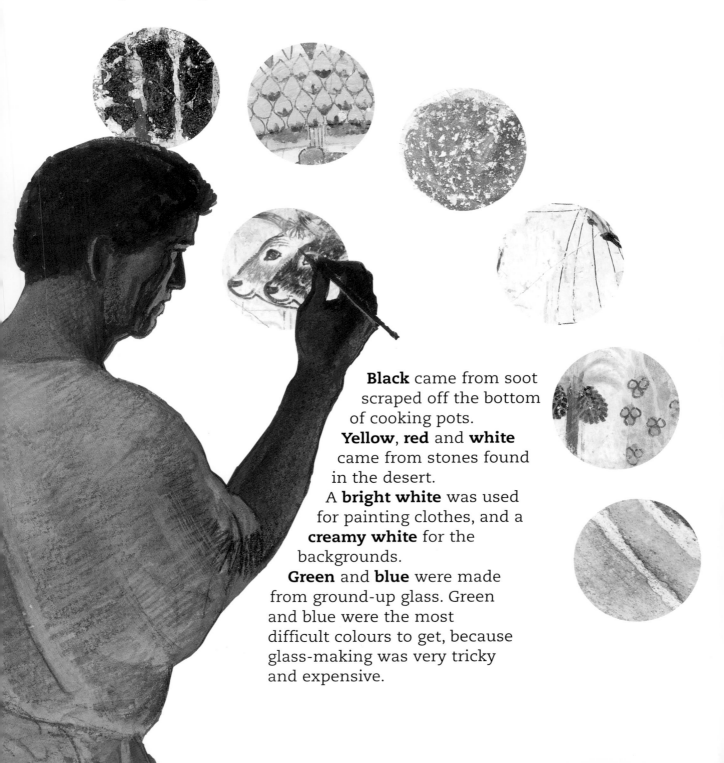

**Black** came from soot scraped off the bottom of cooking pots.

**Yellow**, **red** and **white** came from stones found in the desert.

A **bright white** was used for painting clothes, and a **creamy white** for the backgrounds.

**Green** and **blue** were made from ground-up glass. Green and blue were the most difficult colours to get, because glass-making was very tricky and expensive.

More colours were made by mixing paints together.

Red mixed with black made brown.

Red mixed with white made pink.

Black mixed with white made grey.

The artists used lines and dots of colour to show different kinds of surfaces.

**The scales on a fish.**

**A duck's feathers.**

**The soft folds of cloth.**

**The fur of Nebamun's cat.**

In the floor of Nebamun's tomb-chapel a secret entrance opened into a shaft. The shaft led straight down to the burial chamber. Nebamun knew that after he died his body would be placed in the burial chamber with some of his belongings. Then the shaft would be filled, and the entrance hidden. Noone wanted robbers to find a way down into the chamber and steal the things that lay buried with Nebamun.

Statues of Nebamun and his wife were placed in an alcove at the back of the tomb-chapel. Nebamun's family and friends could visit and leave offerings of food and drink at the feet of the statues.

**Nebamun's tomb probably looked something like this, but no-one knows for certain.**

the statues

shaft

burial chamber

tomb-chapel
outer room

omb-chapel
nner room

# The 'city of the dead'

The tombs of important people filled the hills and valleys to the west of the city of Thebes. It was like a 'city of the dead'.

Some of the tombs were robbed almost straight away. Some were damaged by people who did not like the tomb owners. Much, much later many of the tombs were lived in by the local people. Egypt is a very hot country and the tombs were cool, ready-made homes. The paintings inside the tombs were bumped and scraped. Smoke from fires blackened the colours. Bits of plaster fell off the walls.

Around two hundred years ago a few people began to collect and

sell paintings from the tombs. This saved some of the paintings from being lost, but many paintings were damaged when they were removed.

There are paintings from the tombs in many museums. People study the paintings to find out about ancient Egypt. Almost everything we know about ancient Egypt comes from tombs.

Some of the paintings from Nebamun's tomb were brought to London. They have been in the British Museum, admired as great treasures, ever since. Experts in the Museum have been working on the paintings. Much new information has been discovered as the team of experts cleaned and cared for these precious paintings.

Each piece of a painting, however tiny, came from a larger painting. Each larger painting once belonged with all the paintings in a tomb. Putting the pieces together is like a jigsaw puzzle. Lots of pieces are missing, lost for ever.

**These are the hills outside Thebes. The doors in the hillside lead to tombs. Many of the tombs are badly ruined. Some tombs can be visited, but it is hard work protecting the paintings still inside. Even the breath from tourists can damage the paintings.**

**The people who found Nebamun's tomb and collected some of the paintings around 200 years ago did not say exactly where the tomb was. Nebamun's tomb has not been seen since. Perhaps it was broken into and destroyed. Or – perhaps – it is still here somewhere, covered by sand and stones.**

13

# The meaning of the paintings

Egyptian paintings always have a meaning. People read the paintings, like stories.

The Egyptians believed that they would go on living after they died. The paintings in Nebamun's tomb-chapel showed all the things that Nebamun wanted in his life after death. Some of the paintings showed the kinds of things that he looked forward to doing in his life after death. Some of them showed what he had enjoyed doing while he was still alive, and working in the Temple at Thebes.

Egyptian paintings are works of art, created to be seen and enjoyed. But they were also meant to last for ever, just as Nebamun hoped to live for ever in his life after death, and to be remembered for ever.

**This tomb-chapel was dug into a rocky hillside on the west bank of the Nile at Thebes, about the same time as Nebamun's. It was made for Nakht, who worked for the same temple as Nebamun. The paintings show men and women bringing offerings of food and drink, and ploughing and harvesting grain in the fields.**

# Hunting in the marshes

This painting comes from Nebamun's tomb-chapel. It shows Nebamun standing in a boat, wearing a black wig and a collar of beads. His wife Hatshepsut stands behind him, wearing her best dress. Their daughter picks a lotus flower from the water. His cat helps catch birds.

Nebamun is very happy. He is hunting birds in the marshes. This is one of the things that he hoped to do in his life after death.

But this painting has a secret. The clue is the piece of thin, straight stick in front of Nebamun's boat.

**The hieroglyphs say that Nebamun is enjoying himself, looking at good things.**

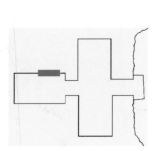

# A secret and a mystery

The painting of Nebamun hunting birds in the marshes was once two times bigger. In the missing half Nebamun stands in his boat with his wife and his son, spearing fish. The thin stick is really the end of Nebamun's long spear, as he thrusts it into a fish. Two pieces from the painting of Nebamun spearing fish were photographed many years ago. But no-one has seen the pieces for many years.

**The complete painting might have looked like this on the wall of Nebamun's tomb-chapel. The missing parts have been drawn in. The two pieces known from photographs are shown in yellow.**

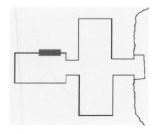

# Food and drink

Many paintings in Nebamun's tomb-chapel show tables piled with good things to eat. Servants carry more food. Nebamun believed that he would need food and drink in his life after death.

Experts have used every scrap of colour and dot and line to work out what the missing pieces in some of the paintings might have looked like.

In Nebamun's garden there are trees to rest under and fruit to eat. The pool is full of fish. A goddess in the tree offers fruit to Nebamun, who would have been sitting at the end of the pool.

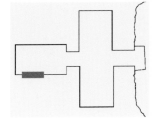

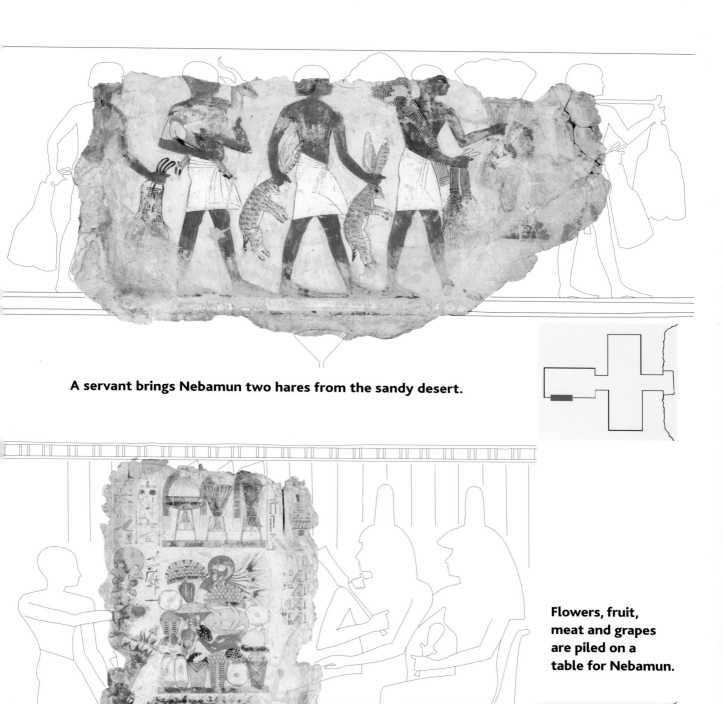

A servant brings Nebamun two hares from the sandy desert.

Flowers, fruit, meat and grapes are piled on a table for Nebamun.

# The party

Some of the paintings show Nebamun enjoying himself at a big party with his family and friends.

All the guests are dressed in their best clothes. They are wearing black wigs and lots of jewellery. The cones balanced on their heads are made of fat mixed with a sweet-smelling scent.

As the fat melts it drips down over their bodies. Servant girls dance, and give drinks to guests. A lady looks straight out of the painting, playing the pipes. Her curly hair sways in time to the music.

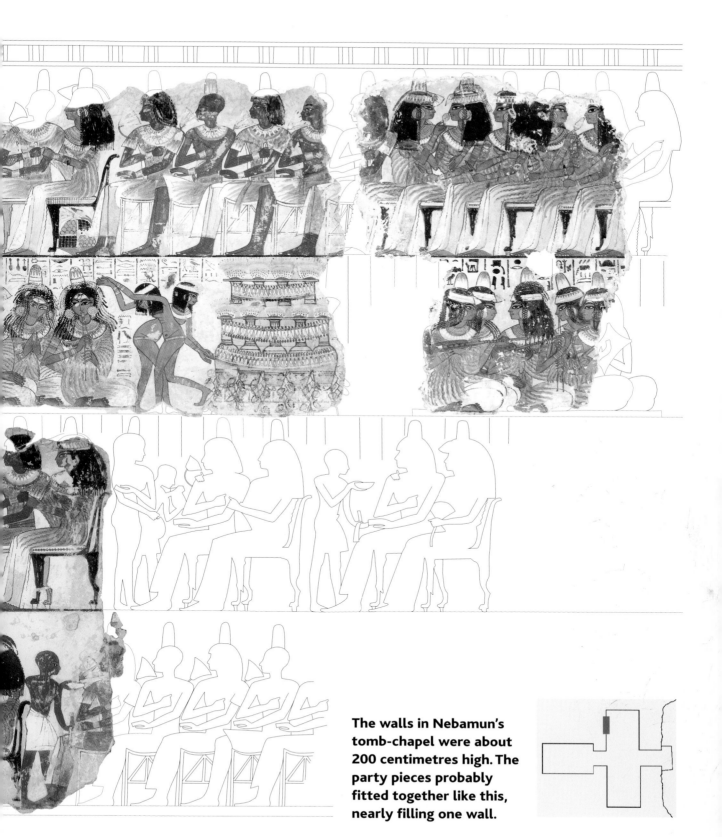

The walls in Nebamun's tomb-chapel were about 200 centimetres high. The party pieces probably fitted together like this, nearly filling one wall.

# Inspecting the geese and cattle

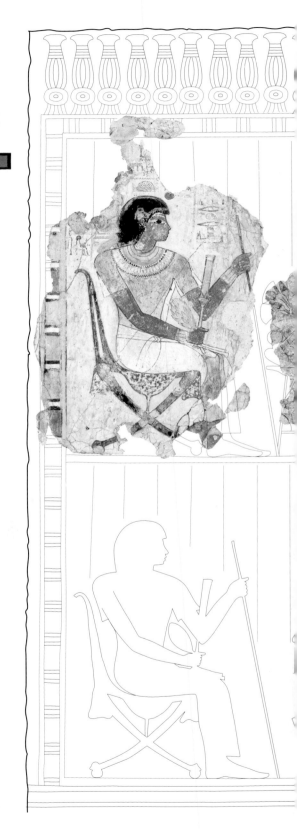

**N**ebamun was in charge of many farms. In this painting he sits listening while a man reads to him. The man is a scribe, so he has a wooden case for his pens under his arm. The wooden chests behind him hold rolls of Egyptian paper, called papyrus.

The scribe calls out the number of geese. Above his head there are spaces for hieroglyphs. Egyptian artists did not like empty spaces in their pictures. But the artists painting Nebamun's pictures worked very fast, and sometimes they left bits out.

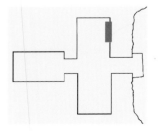

'Sit,' the man with the stick orders the kneeling workers, 'and don't talk!'

The man with a rope in his hand standing amongst the cattle calls out 'Come on, hurry up, do not speak ...'

# Inspecting the fields and farms

Nebamun and his assistants are inspecting the farms. Their chariots and drivers wait for them, in the shade of a tree.

An old farmer checks the boundary stone marking the edge of a field of wheat. He is not an important person, so he has been painted as he would be in real life, balding, and a bit plump.

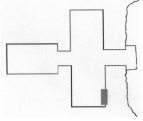

# Egyptian ideas about painting

The most important person in an Egyptian painting is always painted to look bigger than anyone else. So Nebamun looks much bigger than the rest of his family. His skin is a different colour.

Nebamun looks young, slim and healthy in all the pictures of him, although he may have been quite old when they were painted. Men are nearly always handsome in Egyptian paintings, and women are young and beautiful. Important people look the way they wanted to be, not the way they really were.

People in Egyptian paintings are nearly always painted with ...

**their head sideways**

**their shoulders front on**

**their waist sideways**

**their legs and feet sideways**

**one eye front on.**

**But sometimes people do look straight out of the paintings, like the flute-player with the swaying hair at the party.**

# The tomb of Nebamun

About thirty years after Nebamun was buried, the young king Tutankhamun died. His tomb was not robbed. Very unusually, the treasures buried with Tutankhamun survived.

Nebamun had no royal treasures, but he would have wanted his special things buried with him when he died. One day Nebamun's tomb might be found again. The rest of the paintings might still be on the walls of the tomb-chapel. Perhaps Nebamun's burial chamber was never robbed. Nebamun might still be lying undisturbed, surrounded by all the things important to him.

These objects come from the burial chambers of people who lived about the same time as Nebamun. Perhaps Nebamun had beautiful things like these in his tomb.

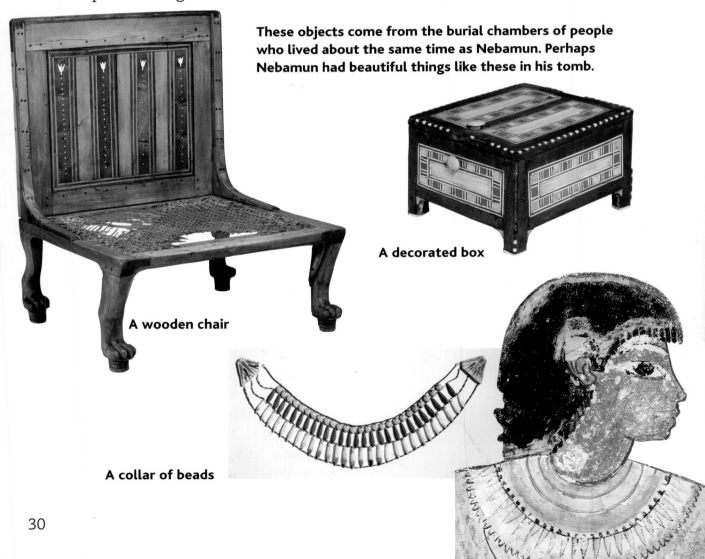

A wooden chair

A decorated box

A collar of beads

**A British Museum conservator works carefully on the banquet scene.**

**Two loaves of bread in a basket**

Nebamun wasn't very rich. He wasn't very important. But somehow he managed to get the best paintings so far found from ancient Egypt as decorations for his tomb-chapel.

Now, the paintings from Nebamun's tomb are admired around the world. Experts at the British Museum have spent years conserving and restoring their fragile surfaces so that visitors can see them displayed once more. And Nebamun, the accountant from the Temple of Amun in Thebes, is famous, after all.

# Index